Created by Wild Pages Press 2017

Made in the USA
Middletown, DE
17 June 2021

42467310R00086